LAMDA
KNOWLEDGE
MATTERS
A practical guide to assist with the theory requirements in LAMDA Examinations

Volume 3

KNOWLEDGE MATTERS Volume 3

Previously published as *The Discussion*: 1996, 2000, 2004 and
Knowledge Matters: 2009, 2014
This edition first published in 2019 by the
London Academy of Music and Dramatic Art
155 Talgarth Road, London W14 9DA
Tel: +44 (0)208 834 0530
www.lamda.ac.uk

Copyright © LAMDA Ltd 2019

Edited by Vinota Karunasaagarar

LAMDA Ltd is hereby identified as author of this publication in accordance with
section 77 of the Copyright, Designs and Patents Act 1988.

A catalogue record for this book is available from the British Library.

Printed by: Hobbs the Printers Ltd, Totton, Hampshire, SO40 3WX
Concept design and layout: Neil Sutton, Cambridge Design Consultants
Illustrations by Neil Sutton
Original diagrams by Lucy Atkinson

ISBN: 978-0-9932443-1-5

Contents

Foreword

As a recent graduate of the London Academy of Music and Dramatic Arts (LAMDA) Foundation Degree in Professional Acting, it is a great pleasure and honour to have been invited to write this foreword for *Knowledge Matters (volume 3)*. It is also somewhat surreal, as not too long ago I was completing my own LAMDA Graded Examinations in Acting, Grade 8, at school. Since leaving LAMDA, I have gone on to work for the Royal Shakespeare Company and have performed in short dramas, television shows and film.

This book is designed to help with the theory elements of LAMDA Examinations. It will assist you in your studies by exploring how to select pieces and by considering the importance of plot, character, themes and figures of speech to a presentation or performance. This book also delves into performance techniques and understanding how your voice works.

In a latter chapter, to provide assistance for Learners performing from Shakespeare's work, the book also looks at the Shakespearean sonnet, Shakespeare's style of writing and his use of language. This is something that is of importance, as I grew up thinking Shakespeare wasn't for me, although a part of me truly enjoyed it. I had always loved the rhythm of the language, although I didn't fully understand it. I appreciated the powerful imagery, although I couldn't always interpret it. And though I could relate to the narrative of each character, I wasn't sure how to approach performance. I believe the relevant chapters of this book will help fill in these gaps for Learners studying Shakespeare, as the beauty of Shakespeare is in the 'doing'. I was once told that I may never perform in a Shakespearean play. Within the first year of my professional career, I had played the part of Ophelia in *Hamlet*, Cordelia in *King Lear* and Guiderius in *Cymbeline* for the Royal Shakespeare Company. No one should be told that Shakespeare isn't for them, as Shakespeare's writing is accessible to everyone. Within Shakespeare's abundant work, there is no theme in life that has not been touched upon, so if you can understand what it is to be human, then you can understand the transcendent magic of Shakespeare.

This book will assist you in studying for your LAMDA Examinations by providing a greater understanding of how to respond to the knowledge requirements of the syllabi, and in turn will aid you with your Performance.

Natalie Simpson

Ian Charleson Award (2017 and 2016)
LAMDA Foundation Degree in Professional Acting (2015)
LAMDA Graded Examinations in Acting, Grade 8 (2008)

Thanks

LAMDA would like to thank all of the contributors who assisted with this and the previous versions of this book: Clarissa Aykroyd, Mia Ball, Paul Bench, Faye Carmichael, Jacque Emery, Jeffrey Grenfell-Hill, Mark Gregson, Greg Hamerton, Vivien Helibron, Linda Macrow, Priscilla Morris, Ann Newson, Stephen Owen, Paul Ranger, John Rhys Thomas, The Voice Care Network UK, Catherine Weate, Amanda Wheeler and Christina Williams.

Introduction

We have called this book *Knowledge Matters* because knowledge of interpretative skills, technical skills and literature is the foundation for any performance or presentation. This book includes useful information for those teaching / preparing for LAMDA Examinations and for teachers and students of communication and performance. This book should be used in conjunction with other information books and teaching resources.

The Knowledge section

The set knowledge questions have been designed to introduce Learners to the technical aspects of performing. The Learner's knowledge is tested in discussion with the Examiner after the Learner has performed their chosen selections. Questioning is more formal in the higher grades as the set knowledge requirements increase in technical difficulty.

The Knowledge section has its own Learning Outcome(s) (LO) and related Assessment Criteria (AC).

The Examiner will initiate the discussion and the Learner will be encouraged to respond. This should evolve into a two-way exchange between the Examiner and the Learner, during which the Learner will be given every opportunity to share their knowledge.

There is a time limit for the Knowledge section and Learners must be prepared to discuss all aspects of the requirements for the grade being assessed.

The Examiner will base their questions on the set knowledge requirements printed in the relevant syllabus. This information should be made available to the Learner by the Teacher so that the Learner is fully prepared and is able to discuss the relevant theory with confidence.

Practical application

This book has been designed to help the Learner to understand and use background knowledge and techniques required to give a creative, enhanced performance.

Practical application of the knowledge learnt and understood will lead to a greater enjoyment in performance. It is, therefore, important that the Learner relates the set knowledge to their performance, as much as possible, in their responses.

The content of this book will enable Learners to appreciate the need for unity between knowledge, creativity and presentation.

Selecting pieces – verse and prose

The fundamental differences between verse and prose

Whatever you read, whether it's a book, newspaper article or magazine, the text is written as verse or prose. It is important to know the difference between verse and prose, and Learners should be able to give a detailed reply, setting out how they can tell the difference.

Prose is the usual form of written and spoken language. In English, words flow continuously across the page and are broken into sentences and paragraphs. Prose writing usually follows a logical sequence and a grammatical order.

Verse is often immediately recognisable on the page because the words are arranged into patterns. Verse may be broken up into stanzas, but this is not essential. Verse often has little grammatical order. Insignificant but grammatically necessary words may be omitted and the accepted word order changed. In some modern verse, there is little or no punctuation and even a lack of capital letters. Verse may also make more use of figures of speech, such as similes and metaphors, than prose. Verse often rhymes at line endings.

Examples of different verse patterns:

Aunt Jennifer's tigers prance across a screen,
Bright topaz denizens of a world of green.
They do not fear the men beneath the tree;
They pace in sleek chivalric certainty.

   Aunt Jennifer's Tigers
   by Adrienne Rich (1929–2012)

Flying by
on the winged-wheels
of their heels

Two teenage earthbirds
zig-zagging
down the street

   Roller Skaters
   by Grace Nichols

As we

embrace   resist

the future   the present   the past

we work   we struggle   we begin   we fail

to understand   to find   to unbraid   to accept   to question

the grief   the grief   the grief   the grief

we shift   we wield   we bury

into light   as ash

across our faces

Obligations 2
by Layli Long Soldier

Verse and **prose** both possess rhythm but verse rhythm is more distinct. Rhythm is the beat or pulse you can hear when you say the words. Sometimes the rhythm is arranged in a regular pattern of stressed and unstressed syllables, which is known as **metre**. Verse rhythm can be very strong and easy to feel, or quite gentle and subtle.

Some examples of verse with a strong metrical rhythm are:

Loving words clutch crimson roses,
Rude words sniff and pick their noses,
Sly words come dressed up as foxes,
Short words stand on cardboard boxes,
Common words tell jokes and gabble,
Complicated words play Scrabble,

The Word Party
by Richard Edwards

Faster than fairies, faster than witches,
Bridges and houses, hedges and ditches;
And charging along like troops in a battle,
All through the meadows the horses and cattle:

From a Railway Carriage
by Robert Louis Stevenson (1850–1894)

Verse examples can be found in any of the LAMDA Verse and Prose anthologies.

The meaning of the words

To understand the whole of a poem you must know the meanings of all the words. If you are uncertain of any words, do not guess their meaning but look them up in a dictionary. Some words have more than one meaning and you can only tell which is correct from the way the word is used within the surrounding text.

The general content of the verse selections

When you have chosen your poems, explore the meaning of them. It is important to understand them as a whole. For example:

- Do they paint a picture?
- Do they tell a story?
- What are the poems saying?

Content and mood of the verse selections

Content is the subject matter that is being dealt with in the verse or prose extract. Mood is the emotion behind the words of the text.

To prepare, you should look at the way the pieces are written.

For example, you could compare two poems and ask the following questions:

- Are they shaped differently on the page?
- Do they have a strong rhythm?
- Do they both use rhyme?
- What is the mood of each poem?
- Is the mood different in the two poems?
- Do the poems tell a story?
- Are the poems descriptive?
- Are the poems sad?
- Are the poems humorous?
- Are the poems scary, atmospheric or cheerful?

You may also enjoy and comment on the sounds of the words in each poem.

For your examination, it is a good idea to select two pieces of verse that differ in either theme or mood so that you are able to show some contrast when you perform them.

Content and mood of the prose selections

When you have read your book, answer these questions:

- What happens in the story?
- Where and when is the story set?
- Do you have a favourite part of the story (and why)?
- How does the extract you are performing fit into the story as a whole?
- What is the mood of the extract you are performing?
- Does the mood change during the extract?

When discussing your book with the Examiner, remember to answer the questions as fully as possible while being concise.

Summary

VERSE	PROSE
LANGUAGE	
• Heightened form of the written and spoken language • Insignificant but grammatically necessary words may be omitted and the accepted word order changed • In some modern verse, there is little or no punctuation • May make more use of figures of speech, such as similes and metaphors • Often rhymes at line endings.	• Usual form of written and spoken language • Usually follows a logical sequence and a grammatical order.
STRUCTURE	
• Recognisable on the page because the words are arranged into patterns • May be broken up into stanzas but this is not essential.	• Words flow continuously across the page and are broken into sentences and paragraphs.
RHYTHM	
• Rhythm is more distinct • Sometimes the rhythm is arranged in a regular pattern of stressed and unstressed syllables • Rhythm can be very strong and easy to feel or quite gentle and subtle.	• The rhythm in prose is random and follows no specific pattern • It is a form of language that exhibits a natural sense of the flow of speech and grammatical structure.
SOURCES (FOUND IN)	
• Poetry books • Faith writing • Greetings cards • Plays.	• Novels • Newspapers • Magazines • Diaries • Information and textbooks.

Continued on next page ▶

SELECTING PIECES – VERSE AND PROSE

13

VERSE	PROSE
EXAMPLE	
The crocodile, with cunning smile, sat in the dentist's chair. He said, "Right here and everywhere my teeth require repair." The dentist's face was turning white. He quivered, quaked and shook. He muttered, "I suppose I'm going to have to take a look." *The Dentist and the Crocodile* by Roald Dahl (1916–1990)	A cunning crocodile went to see the dentist. After the crocodile sat in the dentist's chair he told the dentist that all his teeth had to be repaired. The dentist, who was nervous about looking inside a crocodile's mouth, reluctantly agreed.

Plot and character

Plot of the book/play

The plot is a narrative of events with emphasis on cause and effect – what happened, and why? It is the way that a story is arranged. Important information can be withheld from the reader or the story might not be told in chronological order. For example, in the novel *The Life of Pi* by Yann Martel, the main character, Pi, is on a lifeboat with a hyena, a zebra, an orangutan and a tiger. But it is only at the end of the novel that the reader learns how these animals came to be on board the lifeboat with Pi.

E M Forster (1879–1970) defined the difference between a story and a plot:

A story is a narrative of events in chronological order. A plot is a narrative of events with the emphasis on causality.

Chapters *Themes* and *Figures of speech* can help you understand the plot of the book or play you choose.

Choice of character

When you have read your book/play, think about the character that the extract focuses on and ask the following questions:

- Why did you choose this extract/character?
- Is your chosen character a main character in the story?
- What does the character look like?
- How does the character view themselves?
- What happens to the character during the course of the book/play, and why?

The character's reason for speaking

To understand why the character is speaking, consider factors such as:
- Who is the character?
- What is the character's role in the play?
- What is occurring at the time of the speech?
- What is the character doing?
- Where is the character at the time of the speech?
- Who is the character speaking to?
- What are the character's emotions during the speech?
- How does the character's use of language convey what they're saying?
- What occurs after the speech ends?

The relationship between two or more characters

If there are other characters in the scene or you are performing a duologue ask questions such as the following:
- What do the characters say about each other?
- What do other people say about the characters?
- How do the characters relate to each other?
- How do the characters interact with each other?
- How do the characters develop or change, and why?
- How do the characters' relationships with each other develop or change, and why?

Understanding the intentions of the author can help you to understand the character you choose to play. Chapters *Themes* and *Figures of speech* can assist you with this, and chapters *The voice* and *Performance* will help you to deliver a sound performance.

Analysing the text

This is useful to provide a greater understanding of the text that you are to perform.

Analysing the text requires an understanding of the text that you have chosen, together with the ability to concisely discuss it in detail – look at the text and subtext of the book as a whole, examine the key themes, underlying themes, details of characters and important events within it.

Filling out a table will help you to analyse the text.

Sample table to help analyse text:

PROSE ANALYSIS GRID	
Author	
Key facts about author	
Period and style of writing	
Other books by author	
Book title	
General outline of plot	
Key moments within the book	
Key characters	
Main themes	
Underlying/secondary themes (subtext)	
Interesting quotations from the book	
Personal evaluation of the book	

Themes

Themes are related to plot. A theme is a recurring idea or subject in the novel. It may be broad (love) or specific (the effect of immigration on a particular character). Themes unite the characters, events and structure. For example, in *Pride and Prejudice* by Jane Austen (1775–1817) the characters in the story are involved in various themes, including: love, marriage, greed and adventure. Themes can also be found in poetry; for example, in the poem *Less, much less* by Moniza Alvi, a theme of the poem is someone saying goodbye.

Exploring a theme does not necessarily mean coming to any firm conclusion about it. This is shown in the novel *Picnic at Hanging Rock* by Joan Lindsay (1896–1984). The novel is about the disappearance of students from a girl's boarding school during a day trip to Hanging Rock. At the end of the novel there is no resolution for the reader, as it does not have an ending – the final chapter of the novel was removed prior to publication – and the reader does not discover what happened to the girls.

Subtext (can also be referred to as *underlying themes*)

Subtext is the *internal* world. It is the hidden meaning involving knowledge, emotion and motivation. For example, in the novel *Animal Farm* by George Orwell (1903–1950), on the surface, the story is about animals acting and reacting to each other, but the subtext (underlying theme) refers to the behaviour of human beings.

Specific verse forms

Before performing a poem or sonnet, you should be able to select the appropriate verse form, metre and rhythm that matches your selected piece. Though there are many verse forms to explore, here we will look at three significant verse forms in more detail: blank verse, free verse and sonnet form.

(a) **Blank verse.** Blank verse consists of a succession of unrhymed lines, which have a regular rhythm. It creates a sense of simplicity and directness, perfect for character speech and dramatic performance. The poem *Look to the New Moon* by Mai Der Vang is an example of this:

> *If you must hear   the story*
> *of my turbulent gaze   after waking,*
>
> *the march of my hours   to hermit*
> *into a higher body,   it is that*
>
> *whatever you put   into the Universe*
> *eventually   returns.*

Shakespeare even mentions the term 'blank verse' in Act 2 Scene 2 of *Hamlet*, when Hamlet says:

> *The lady shall say her mind freely − or the*
> *blank verse shall halt for't.*

Sometimes, an occasional change to the rhythm is added in order to create variety. Hermione's trial speech in Act 3 Scene 2 of *The Winter's Tale* is in blank verse but includes a metrical change in the fifth line, which strengthens her sense of innocence:

Since what I am to say, must be but that
Which contradicts my accusation, and
The testimony on my part, no other
But what comes from myself, it shall scarce boot me
To say 'not guilty':

(b) **Free verse**. Free verse possesses a structure but it is much more open and not bound by classical rules such as those found in sonnet form.

Free verse is not necessarily confined to a specific metrical law but uses a rhythm most suitable for the expression of a particular thought and emotion. For example, if the thought or emotion is profound, then the rhythm will move slowly; if the thought or emotion is trivial, then the rhythm will gallop along. A rhythmical unit of free verse is not a line but a stanza, or even the whole poem itself.

Rhyme can be included in free verse but is usually a necessary part of the thought and/or emotion. Free verse came into its own in the early twentieth century with the modernist movement. *The Love Song of J Alfred Prufrock* by T. S. Eliot (1888–1965) is a particularly good example:

Let us go then, you and I,
When the evening is spread out against the sky
Like a patient etherised upon a table;

Out of the Cradle Endlessly Rocking, taken from *Leaves of Grass* by Walt Whitman (1819–1892) is another example:

Till of a sudden,
May-be kill'd, unknown to her mate,
One forenoon the she-bird crouch'd not on the nest,
Nor return'd that afternoon, nor the next,
Nor ever appear'd again.

And thenceforward all summer in the sound of the sea,
And at night, under the full of the moon, in calmer
*   weather,*
Over the hoarse surging of the sea,
Or flitting from brier to brier by day,
I saw, I heard at intervals the remaining one, the he-bird
The solitary guest from Alabama.

A twenty-first-century example of free verse can be seen in
the poem *From "Oil"* by Fatimah Asghar:

My auntie says my people might
*   be Afghani. I draw a ship on the map.*
I write Afghani under its hull. I count
*   all the oceans, blood & not-blood,*
all the people I could be,
*   the whole map, my mirror.*

(c) Sonnet form

- **The Petrarchan or Italian sonnet**. The sonnet form is
  of Italian origin dating back to the Renaissance and was
  used by both Dante and Petrarch. The Petrarchan sonnet
  consists of fourteen lines divided into an octave and a
  sestet. The octave is made up of two quatrains (sets of
  four lines). The sestet is composed of two tercets (sets of
  three lines).

- When the sonnet is written in Italian, the rhyming scheme
  is limited. In the octave only two rhymes are the norm:
  abba abba. Three pairs of rhymes are found in the tercet:
  cde cde.

- The *subject* consists of one idea, which is stated
  boldly (often in universal terms) in the first quatrain and
  developed in the second. A pause then follows. In each
  of the two tercets the subject is again considered but
  particular details are shown. Finally, it is brought to a
  definite and forceful close.

- The Petrarchan sonnet was introduced from Italy into England by Thomas Wyatt and developed by Henry Howard, Earl of Surrey. Difficulties were encountered due to the differences between the two languages and, in order to accommodate the language change, extra rhymes had to be incorporated. A second change in the form was the rearrangement of the sestet in a variety of ways: sometimes the change was in the rhyming scheme, which was altered to *cd cd cd* with the sense continued in the series of three couplets (sets of two lines) instead of spread over two tercets. In England the form became more flexible than in Italy.

An example of the English development of the Petrarchan sonnet is *Upon Westminster Bridge* by William Wordsworth (1770–1850):

> *Earth has not anything to show more fair:*
> *Dull would he be of soul who could pass by*
> *A sight so touching in its majesty:*
> *This city now doth, like a garment, wear*
> *The beauty of the morning; silent, bare,*
> *Ships, towers, domes, theatres, and temples lie*
> *Open unto the fields, and to the sky:*
> *All bright and glittering in the smokeless air.*
> *Never did sun more beautifully steep*
> *In his first splendour, valley, rock, or hill:*
> *Ne'er saw I, never felt, a calm so deep!*
> *The river glideth at his own sweet will:*
> *Dear God! The very houses seem asleep;*
> *And all that mighty heart is lying still!*

Another well known example is *Sonnet 43* (better known as *How Do I Love Thee?*) by Elizabeth Barrett Browning (1806–1861):

> *How do I love thee? Let me count the ways.*
> *I love thee to the depth and breadth and height*
> *My soul can reach, when feeling out of sight*
> *For the ends of being and ideal grace.*
> *I love thee to the level of every day's*
> *Most quiet need, by sun and candle-light.*
> *I love thee freely, as men strive for right;*
> *I love thee purely, as they turn from praise.*
> *I love thee with the passion put to use*
> *In my old griefs, and with my childhood's faith.*
> *I love thee with a love I seemed to lose*
> *With my lost saints. I love thee with the breath,*
> *Smiles, tears, of all my life; and, if God choose,*
> *I shall but love thee better after death.*

- **The Shakespearean sonnet**. William Shakespeare departed from the tightly interlaced model of the Petrarchan sonnet. In its place he used a form which, still consists of an octave and a sestet but with a pause between the two, which breaks into different shapes:
  - the octave is divided into two quatrains, made distinct by the rhyme scheme which runs: *abab cdcd*
  - the sestet consists of a quatrain, *efef*, and a final couplet, *gg*.

This pattern allowed Shakespeare:

- to present an argument in the octave
- to recognise either a development or a contradiction of this in the first four lines of the sestet
- to make a strong concluding statement in the couplet.

This is particularly evident in *Sonnet 97*:

> *How like a winter hath my absence been*
> *From thee, the pleasure of the fleeting year!*
> *What freezings have I felt, what dark days seen,*
> *What old December's bareness everywhere!*
> *And yet this time removed was summer's time,*
> *The teeming autumn big with rich increase*
> *Bearing the wanton burden of the prime,*
> *Like widowed wombs after their lords' decease:*
> *Yet this abundant issue seemed to me*
> *But hope of orphans, and unfathered fruit;*
> *For summer and his pleasures wait on thee,*
> *And thou away, the very birds are mute;*
> > *Or if they sing, 'tis with so dull a cheer*
> > *That leaves look pale, dreading the winter's near.*

Our chapter on *Shakespeare* explores the Shakespearean sonnet in further detail.

Versification

Versification is the art of making verses or the theory of the phonetic structure of verse. In the English language the basic system of versification is known as **accentual-syllabic**. This describes the pattern made between the number of syllables in the line of verse and the accents placed on them. In most English poetry the verse structure is created in this way, by balancing the fixed or varying numbers of syllables in a line with the constant alternation of accented and unaccented syllables in definite, recurring sequences.

Metre and rhythm

English speech rhythm is formed by a combination of weak and strong stresses. English verse rhythm depends upon the arrangement of these stresses into patterns. When that pattern is regular and repeated, it is called **metre**.

One bar or unit of a metrical form is called a **foot**, derived from dancing in Ancient Greece when the foot was raised and set down on the stressed beat of a musical bar.

A metric line is named according to the number of feet:

monometer	=	one foot to a line
dimeter	=	two feet to a line
trimeter	=	three feet to a line
tetrameter	=	four feet to a line
pentameter	=	five feet to a line
hexameter	=	six feet to a line
heptameter	=	seven feet to a line
octometer	=	eight feet to a line

A metric line is also named according to the type of **rhythm** within the unit or bar. In English verse there are two main types: **rising rhythm** and **falling rhythm**.

(a) **Rising rhythm**

Iambus (an iambic foot). An iambic foot consists of an unstressed followed by a stressed syllable:

weak <u>strong</u> | weak <u>strong</u> | weak <u>strong</u> | weak <u>strong</u> | weak <u>strong</u> | (iambic pentameter)

de dum | de dum | de dum | de dum | de dum | (iambic pentameter)

It comes from the Greek word meaning 'to hurl' or 'to throw', used when writers of satire hurled their verse, like a weapon, at their enemies. The rhythm resembles the beating of a human heart and is very close to natural speech patterns. Although we may not be aware of it, everyday conversation frequently falls into an iambic rhythm. For example:

I hope you take the book with you to school.

I <u>hope</u> | you <u>take</u> | the <u>book</u> | with <u>you</u> | to <u>school</u>

The ticket isn't valid for today.

The <u>tick</u> | et <u>is</u> | n't <u>val</u> | id <u>for</u> | to<u>day</u>

This is one reason why Elizabethan dramatists, who were heavily influenced by the metrical forms adopted by the Greek and Latin poets of antiquity, were attracted to it. The forward drive of the iambus also makes it ideal for ongoing narrative.

For example, Romeo speaks in iambic pentameter as he waits below Juliet's window in Act 2 Scene 2 of *Romeo and Juliet*:

But soft, what light through yonder window breaks?

But <u>soft</u>, | what <u>light</u> | through <u>yon</u> | der <u>win</u> | dow <u>breaks?</u>

Notice how the metrical structure of the line gives emphasis to the words 'soft', 'light' and 'breaks'.

- **Anapaest (an anapaestic foot)**. An anapaestic foot consists of two unstressed syllables followed by a stressed syllable:

  de de <u>dum</u> | de de <u>dum</u> | de de <u>dum</u> | de de <u>dum</u> | de de <u>dum</u>

This creates a rapid effect, driving the line of the verse forward, which mirrors the movement. An example can be seen in *The Destruction of Sennacherib* by Lord Byron (1788–1824):

The Assyrian came down like the wolf on the fold;
And his cohorts were gleaming in purple and gold:

The <u>Assyr</u> | ian came <u>down</u> | like the <u>wolf</u> | on the <u>fold</u>;
And his <u>co</u> | horts were <u>gleam</u> | ing in <u>pur</u> | ple and <u>gold</u>:

(b) Falling rhythm

- **Trochee (a trochaic foot)**. A trochaic foot consists of a stressed syllable followed by an unstressed syllable:

  <u>dum</u> de | <u>dum</u> de | <u>dum</u> de | <u>dum</u> de | <u>dum</u> de
  <u>Never</u> | <u>Never</u> | <u>Never</u> | <u>Never</u> | <u>Never</u>

King Lear's response upon discovering his daughter Cordelia dead is captured in the mournful, falling tone of the metre.

Shakespeare often used a trochee at the start of an iambic line, which emphasises the meaning of the first word, as in *Sonnet 27*:

Weary with toil, I haste me to my bed,

<u>Weary</u> | with <u>toil</u>, | I <u>haste</u> | me <u>to</u> | my <u>bed</u>,

- **Dactyl (a dactylic foot).** A dactylic foot consists of a stressed syllable followed by two unstressed syllables:

  <u>dum</u> de de | <u>dum</u> de de | <u>dum</u> de de | <u>dum</u> de de | <u>dum</u> de de

In the following line, spoken by Hamlet in Act 3 Scene 1 of *Hamlet*, the metre places stress on the word 'that', highlighting the reflective nature of the speech and drawing our attention to the 'question'. The use of two lighter syllables in the fourth foot rapidly moves the line forward to 'question':

To be, or not to be, that is the question:

To <u>be</u>, | or <u>not</u> | to be, | <u>that</u> is the | <u>quest</u>ion:

(c) Other rhythms

- **Spondee (a spondaic foot).** A spondaic foot consists of two successive syllables with equal weight:

  | <u>dum</u> <u>dum</u> |

It is usually used in the middle or at the end of a line for extra emphasis. An example can be found in *The Rime of the Ancient Mariner* by Samuel Taylor Coleridge (1772–1834):

Alone, alone, <u>all</u>, <u>all</u> alone,

Alone on a wide, wide sea!

(d) Examples of these feet in English prosody are as follows:

- iambus – a<u>way</u>
- anapaest – incom<u>plete</u>
- trochee – <u>du</u>ty
- dactyl – <u>mer</u>rily
- spondee – <u>old</u> <u>time</u>

(e) Blending of rhythms.

A succession of lines consisting of the same kind of metrical rhythm can be monotonous. Many poets, therefore, combine different rhythms to create interest. Sometimes a poem can pass from rising to falling rhythm and back again. A change in rhythm can bring a change in the meaning or mood; equally, a change in the meaning or mood can bring a change in the rhythm.

(f) **Scansion**. To scan a piece of verse is to go through it line by line, analysing the number of feet and marking the weak and strong stresses. While it is not necessary to scan poems or speeches in detail, it is absolutely imperative that you have a firm grasp of the ways in which poetic structure links with thought and emotion. An understanding of metrical patterning can often provide the key to the meaning of a passage that might at first seem difficult to comprehend. If you know where the stresses fall in a given speech, you will find it easier to understand and communicate the sense of the writing.

It is important that the rules of poetic form are not applied to the exclusion of thought and emotion. Working with the rhythm and metre must be connected to feeling and impulse. Overemphasis of the metre can be to the detriment of the mood and the poet's intention.

Emphasis

Emphasis is when a speaker attaches extra prominence to a particular word or thought. It can be achieved through:

• modulation (varying use of stress, volume, pace, pitch, inflection, tone colour and pausing)
• lengthening individual sounds
• intensity.

For example, dramatic emphasis can be achieved by increasing the intensity of the breath force, building volume and widening the pitch range.

If there is *underemphasis*, speech becomes dull, flat and monotonous. Sometimes, in certain types of humour, it can be used effectively, but this should be thought of as a technique rather than the normal means of communication.

If there is *overemphasis*, speech becomes irritating and tiring to listen to.

Modulation

Modulation refers to the variations in voice and speech used by the speaker to convey meaning, mood and emotion. This includes varying the use of stress, volume, pace, pitch, inflection, tone colour and pausing.

(a) **Stress**

Stress is when prominence is given to a particular word or syllable, usually through a combination of extra breath force, a change in pitch and a lengthening of sound.

- **Word stress.** Every word of more than one syllable has its own stress: for example, <u>dra</u>gon. Some words change meaning according to word stress: for example, <u>sub</u>ject (meaning a course of study) / sub<u>ject</u> (meaning to cause somebody to undergo something unpleasant). Compound words usually bear double stress: for example, <u>home-made</u>

- **Sentence stress.** When words are linked together, word stress changes under the influence of sentence stress. Sentence stress depends on two things:

  The relative importance of words in the sentence, and, therefore, the stress, depends on the context. The more important the word, the stronger its stress. For example:

  Did she give you the book? No, <u>he</u> gave me the book.

  Did you steal the book? No, he <u>gave</u> me the book.

  Is the book hers? No, he gave <u>me</u> the book.

  Did he give you the pen? No, he gave me the <u>book</u>.

  The rhythm and meaning of the sentence can be changed by varying the stress. For example:

  In the <u>dark</u>, dark <u>wood</u> sat a <u>cruel</u> <u>hairy</u> <u>giant</u>.

  In the <u>dark</u>, dark <u>wood</u> sat a <u>cruel</u> hairy <u>giant</u>.

(b) **Volume.** Volume refers to the level of loudness or softness with which words are spoken. There should be constant fluctuations of volume to create a well-modulated delivery, but for most work (especially verse speaking) there should be only the gentlest crescendo (becoming louder) and diminuendo (becoming softer). If too much breath force is used, then shouting will occur. Shouting lacks subtlety and can create vocal problems.

(c) **Pace**. Pace variation is integral to the communication of meaning and mood. There should be constant fluctuations of pace to create a well-modulated delivery.

A slower pace can be achieved by lengthening vowels and prolonging the space between words. Words suggesting size, effort, astonishment and long periods of time can be taken more slowly. Meaningful and emotional passages tend to be taken at a slower pace. A phrase which contains several ideas might be taken more slowly and deliberately than one with a simple idea.

A faster pace can be achieved by shortening vowel sounds and continuant consonants, and shortening the space between words. Quick, easy, little, ordinary things can be taken more rapidly. An increase in pace can also be used to build to a climax. Pace is affected by the distribution of stresses in a phrase. Lighter stressing and a more rhythmical distribution of stresses can be taken at a swifter pace.

(d) **Tempo or rate**. Tempo is the overall rate, or time signature, of the writing. Pace will fluctuate considerably within the limits of the tempo used by the speaker and set by the writer.

(e) **Pitch**. Pitch is the specific level of highness or lowness in a speech note. A higher pitch is often used for lighter and happier thoughts. A lower pitch is often used for sombre and sad thoughts.

(f) **Inflection**. Inflection refers to the rise and fall in pitch of the voice during speech. As the voice rises and falls, it tends to form patterns or tunes. The two most commonly heard tunes are called **falling tune** and **rising tune**.

Falling tune. This is a simple falling pattern where the stressed syllables descend from a higher pitch to a lower one. It tends to be used for:

- complete statements
- commands
- agreement
- aggression
- strong emotion
- questions not requiring a 'yes' or 'no' answer
- end of breath-groups.

Examples using a falling tune:

- We are fortunate to have John Smith spending the day with us.
- Put that on the table.
- I agree with your opinion.

Rising tune. This is also a pattern of descending stressed syllables, but there is a rise of pitch on the last syllable. It tends to be used for:

- doubt
- anxiety
- surprise
- pleading
- threats
- incomplete statements
- questions requiring a 'yes' or 'no' answer
- the end of a single sense-group within a larger breath-group.

Try these examples using a rising tune:

- I'm not too sure about that one.
- Please don't leave me now.
- Would you like to come to the football match?

Inflection reflects our personality, our thoughts and our feelings. Flexible use of inflection will, therefore, reveal subtle changes in our moods. Use of inflection must be unconscious or speech becomes stilted. The speaker should focus on communicating meaning and mood to avoid artificiality.

(g) **Tone colour**. Tone colour refers to the variation of 'light' and 'shade' in the voice. It is the result of various tensions and relaxations in the resonators and other associated muscles but is prompted by the imagination and emotion. The quality of tone, therefore, alters according to the feelings, which helps the listener to recognise the mood of the speaker regardless of the words spoken.

In performance, the tone colour should reflect the mood of the prose or verse, but this must be sincerely imagined or it will sound false.

(h) **Intensity.** Fluctuations in intensity indicate tension and relaxation according to the prevailing mood. A performer should avoid giving a whole performance at a high pitch of intensity because it is too tiring for both the performer and the audience and the value of contrast and sincerity would be lost.

 Now select a piece to perform. Think about when and why you would use the discussed features in the performance of your piece.

Figures of speech

A figure of speech (literary device) is a non-literal expression or one which uses a particular pattern of words for emphasis. Such features are found more commonly in verse than prose, though some are used quite regularly in everyday speech without being recognised for what they are.

Authors use different figures of speech to emphasise what they want to say. By understanding the different figures of speech we can decipher the meaning of the text.

Alliteration

Alliteration is the repetition of an initial consonant. This can produce a striking effect when the poem is spoken aloud. One effective example of the repetition of the 'd' sound is found throughout the poem *Drum Dream Girl* by Margarita Engle:

> *On an island of music*
> *in a city of drumbeats*
> *the drum dream girl*
> *dreamed*

An example of alliteration in prose can be seen in *I Know Why the Caged Bird Sings* by Maya Angelou (1928–2014). The 's' sound is repeated throughout the following passage:

> *Up the aisle, the moans and screams merged with the sickening smell of woollen black clothes worn in summer weather and green leaves wilting over yellow flowers.*

Assonance

Less commonly used than alliteration, assonance is the repetition of a vowel sound, and again it is particularly noticeable when the lines are spoken. Repetition of the short 'u' and 'a' sounds in *The Sea* by Daphne Lister illustrates this:

The waves come
tumbling,
rumbling,
crashing,
dashing the harbour wall...

The poem *Do Not Go Gentle into That Good Night* by Dylan Thomas (1914–1953) provides a good example of alliteration and assonance combined:

Do not go gentle into that good night,
Old age should burn and rave at close of day;
Rage, rage against the dying of the light.

An example of assonance in prose can be seen with the repetition of the 'a' sound in *On the Come Up* by Angie Thomas:

"What's going on, Brianna?" she asks.
I look from her to the phone and back. "What you mean?"
"You were extremely distracted today," she says. "You didn't even do your practice test."
"Yes, I did!" Kinda. A little. Sorta. Not really. Nah

Onomatopoeia

Onomatopoeia is another device that makes particular use of sounds. It refers to those words that make a sound similar to their meaning when spoken aloud. Among the simplest are 'pop' and 'hiss'. There are relatively few words, which really fulfil this criterion, but in poetry there is often an onomatopoeic quality to phrases, which enhance the meaning when spoken. One example is from Judith Nicholls' *Sounds Good*:

> *Sausage sizzles*
> *Crispbreads crack*
> *Hot dog hiss*
> *And flapjacks snap!*

Midnight Cats by Jacqueline Emery (1949–2014) also concentrates on sound:

> *Hissing,*
> *Screeching,*
> *Yowling,*
> *Tearing,*
> *Balls of fur*
> *Rolling with a loud crash!*

Onomatopoeia in prose can be seen in the novel *Operation Gadgetman* by Malorie Blackman:

> *A small red-and-yellow doobry-whatsit <u>whizzed</u> through the open kitchen window and shot over her head.*

Antithesis

Antithesis occurs when a word, phrase or idea is set in opposition to another, resulting in a strong contrast or ambiguity which can often surprise or shock. In its simplest form it is the placing of opposites beside one another, as in *Zebra Question* by Shel Silverstein (1930–1999):

> *Are you noisy with quiet times?*
> *Or are you quiet with noisy times?*

It is quite a dramatic device and was often used by Shakespeare. A more striking and developed example of antithesis can be seen in one of Romeo's speeches from Act 1 Scene 1 of *Romeo and Juliet*:

Here's much to do with hate, but more with love.

Why then, O brawling love, O loving hate,

O anything of nothing first create!

O heavy lightness, serious vanity,

An example of antithesis in prose can be seen in *The Picture of Dorian Gray* by Oscar Wilde (1854–1900):

When we are happy, we are always good, but when we are good, we are not always happy.

Simile

A simile is one of the most commonly used figures of speech, likening one thing to another thing. One simple example is found in the opening lines of the poem *A Birthday* by Christina Rossetti (1830–1894):

My heart is like a singing bird

Whose nest is in a water'd shoot;

My heart is like an apple-tree

Whose boughs are bent with thickset fruit;

Another example of a simile is found in Seni Seneviratne's poem *Cinnamon Roots*:

But Portugal, travels East to an island that falls, like

a teardrop, from the tip of India. Finds your soft sweetness,

wraps it in hard cash, grows rich on your rarity,

founding a spice trade, that deals in blood.

You can always recognise a simile by the use of the words 'like' or 'as'. An example of a simile in prose can be seen in *Jane Eyre* by Charlotte Brontë (1816–1855) where simile is used to describe the contents of a room:

> *Scarcely less prominent was an ample cushioned easy-chair near the head of the bed, also white, with a footstool before it; and looking, as I thought, like a pale throne*

Personification

Personification is where inanimate things are endowed with human qualities. In *Ode to the West Wind*, Percy Bysshe Shelley (1792–1822) addresses the west wind as if it is a person:

> *O wild West Wind, thou breath of Autumn's being,*
> *Thou, from whose unseen presence the leaves dead*
> *Are driven, like ghosts from an enchanter fleeing,*
>
> *Yellow, and black, and pale, and hectic red,*
> *Pestilence-stricken multitudes: O thou,*
> *Who chariotest to their dark wintry bed*
>
> *The winged seeds, where they lie cold and low,*
> *Each like a corpse within its grave, until*
> *Thine azure sister of the Spring shall blow*
>
> *Her clarion o'er the dreaming earth, and fill*
> *(Driving sweet buds like flocks to feed in air)*
> *With living hues and odours plain and hill:*
>
> *Wild Spirit, which art moving everywhere;*
> *Destroyer and preserver; hear, oh hear!*

Another good example of personification in verse can be seen in the poem *Truth* by Gwendolyn Brooks (1917–2000), where the sun is referred to as a person:

And if sun comes

How shall we greet him?

Shall we not dread him,

Shall we not fear him

After so lengthy a

Session with shade?

An example of personification in prose can be found in Margaret Atwood's *The Handmaid's Tale*:

Light pours down upon it from the sun, true, but also heat rises, from the flowers themselves, you can feel it: like holding your hand an inch above an arm, a shoulder. It breathes, in the warmth, breathing itself in.

Metaphor

A metaphor describes one thing in terms of another, creating a comparison. An example of metaphor can be seen in the poem *"Hope" is the thing with feathers* by Emily Dickinson (1830–1886):

"Hope" is the thing with feathers -

That perches in the soul -

And sings the tune without the words -

And never stops - at all –

Some metaphors are extended through an entire piece of writing. In the poem *Hard Frost* by Andrew Young (1885–1971) the frost is seen as an army and the image is sustained through the whole poem:

But vainly the fierce frost

Interns poor fish, ranks trees in an armed host,

Hangs daggers from house-eaves

And on the windows ferny ambush weaves;

In the long war grown warmer

The sun will strike him dead and strip his armour.

In the play *The Crucible* by Arthur Miller (1915–2005), the play itself is a metaphor. This is known as an extended metaphor, as the metaphor is present for the duration of the play – the play is about the Salem witch trials, which occurred in America in the 1690s, but the playwright compares this to the hunt for Communists in America in the 1950s.

The voice

An understanding of how your voice works will help you to develop your ability to project your voice. This can be achieved by exploring breathing, voice and speech production.

Breathing

'Breath is fundamental to life. It is also fundamental to producing voice. Because breathing is an involuntary activity, we seldom give it a thought unless it is difficult or painful. But if we hear that our voice is too soft, fades away or won't carry, we need to consider how we breathe.'

(From *More Care for Your Voice* by the Voice Care Network UK)

There are numerous bones and muscles involved in the breathing process.

(a) **Bones**. The spine is made up of a series of vertebrae. The twelve pairs of thoracic vertebrae curve around to the front of the chest forming the ribcage. Seven pairs join with the sternum. Three pairs join with the seventh and two pairs are 'floating' (unattached). You can feel the definition of the ribs with your fingers.

(b) **Muscles**. The *intercostal muscles* are situated between the ribs (inter = between, costal = ribs). The *diaphragm* is a dome-shaped muscle dividing the chest and the abdomen. It is attached to the lower edges of the ribcage, the point of the sternum and, at the back, the vertebrae. The *abdominal muscles* form part of the abdominal cavity and help to control the movement of the diaphragm.

(c) **Breathing in**. When we breathe in, the intercostal muscles contract and move the ribs slightly upwards and outwards. The diaphragm, which is attached to the ribs, moves in response to this action, flattening out. This creates more space inside the chest, giving the lungs room to expand. As the lungs expand, the air pressure reduces and air immediately flows in through the nose or mouth in order to equalise the pressure. The abdominal muscles release and the lungs fill with air.

(d) **Breathing out**. We then exhale. The muscles converge simultaneously to support the release of the breath. The abdominal muscles contract, the diaphragm rises and the ribcage returns to its original position through the relaxation of the intercostals. The lungs are compressed, and air flows out through the nose and mouth, powered by the abdominal muscles.

(e) **Support**. Your Teacher may have given you a direction to 'support your voice'. This means having just the right amount of pressure from the abdominal muscles to create just the right amount of breath force for the sound you want to use. For example, if you want to project your voice across a large space or to sustain a long phrase, then you will need a more consistent pressure from the abdominal muscles.

Relaxation exercises, followed by breathing exercises, will help you with this process. When you practise a breathing exercise, place your hands on your lower abdomen and centre your attention there. This will help the abdominal muscles to release on the in-breath and contract on the out-breath. Taking breath from your 'centre' (an imaginary point inside your body below your navel) will also help you to relax and release the sound more freely and easily.

(f) **Clavicular breathing**. This type of breathing is to be avoided. It involves moving the ribs upwards but not outwards when breathing in, holding air in the upper lungs and raising the shoulders. This sometimes happens when the body is tense, putting strain on the vocal folds. Make sure that your spine is lengthened and your shoulders, neck and jaw are free from tension.

Voice production

'Voice begins with an impulse from the brain. It is stimulated by an intention to speak or sing. Two elements produce voice – a flow of air and vibration.

The air flows from breath. Air is taken in through the mouth or nose, passes down the trachea (or wind-pipe) and into the lungs. It is drawn there by the contraction of the dome-like diaphragm. As the diaphragm relaxes, the abdominal muscles work to return breath up the trachea.

The larynx (or voice box) is located in the upper part of the trachea. Its primary biological function is to serve as a protective valve for the air-way. When we use our voice, we close two bands of muscular tissue in the larynx – the vocal folds (or cords) – across the air flow. The out-breath causes the edges of the folds to vibrate, generating sound, in a manner similar to that of air escaping from the neck of a balloon as it deflates. The edges of the vocal cords are quite short – 15–20 mm – and their vibration is extremely rapid. Depending on age, sex, health and the note pitched, the vocal folds may open and close between 60 and 1000 times per second.'

(From *More Care for Your Voice* by the Voice Care Network UK)

Figure 1: The larynx (from the side)

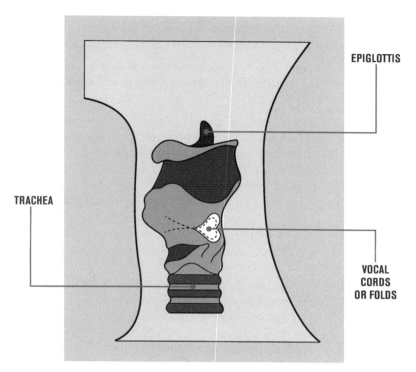

EPIGLOTTIS

TRACHEA

VOCAL
CORDS
OR FOLDS

Figure 2: The larynx (from above)

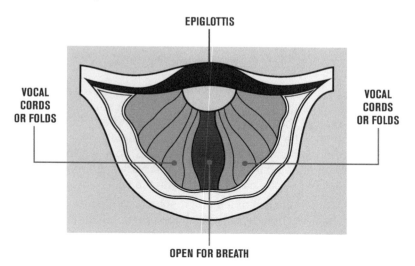

EPIGLOTTIS

VOCAL
CORDS
OR FOLDS

VOCAL
CORDS
OR FOLDS

OPEN FOR BREATH

Basic speech production: Resonance

Resonance is the amplification of sound achieved through vibration. The quality of the sound is deep, full, and reverberating.

Vocal resonance refers to the amplification of sound waves as they pass through the hollow spaces of the pharynx, mouth and nose.

The note created in the vocal folds is carried by the breath through various hollow spaces: the **pharynx** (or pharyngeal resonator), the **mouth** (or oral resonator) and the **nose** (or nasal resonator). The note is strengthened, amplified and given texture as it travels through these spaces.

(a) **The pharynx (pharyngeal resonator).** This is the long, muscular tube that extends upwards from the larynx, ending at the back part of the oral and nasal cavities. It is the first resonating space through which the note must pass on its way to the mouth and nose.

   The pharynx can change its shape and size, which affects the quality of the sound produced. It increases in size during a yawn and decreases in size when the throat or neck is tense.

try this Hold a yawn in your throat and count 'one, two, three' at the same time. You will hear a sound with too much pharyngeal resonance.

(b) **The mouth (oral resonator).** Each of the many parts of the mouth has a role to play in producing resonance.

   The lower jaw forms the floor of the oral resonator and is attached to the facial bones by hinge joints.

   The tongue lies on the floor of the oral resonator, rooted in the front wall of the pharynx. It is capable of intricate and rapid movements. The movement is centred in different areas: the tip (point of the tongue), the blade (underneath the upper tooth ridge), the front (underneath the hard palate), the centre (partly underneath the hard palate and partly underneath the soft palate) and the back (underneath the soft palate).

   The lips form the exit of the oral resonator at the free edges of the mouth and grip, direct and shape the breath stream.

The hard palate is an arched bone structure, separating the oral cavity from the nasal cavities, forming the roof of the mouth.

The soft palate forms the back third of the roof of the mouth, continuing from the curve of the hard palate. The back edge is free and can move up and down. Its movement controls the flow of air through the nose or mouth, like a trap door.

When breathing naturally through the nose, the soft palate is relaxed and droops down into the mouth, which leaves the passage to the nose free. When there is an impulse to speak, the soft palate contracts upwards, blocking the passage to the nose, so that the air and sound flow through the mouth.

Say the long vowel sound 'h' with your lower jaw dropped at its most natural point. Continue saying the sound and raise your lower jaw slowly. As the lower jaw comes up, your lips will move closer together and the tongue might move towards the hard palate. You will hear a sound without much oral resonance.

Breath carries the sound from the pharynx into the mouth. If the breath force is strong enough, the sound will bounce off the hard palate and out through the lips. This is called forward resonance.

If the breath force is too weak to reach the hard palate, it may pitch on to the soft palate, which will make the sound difficult to project.

The mouth is capable of assuming a wide range of sizes and shapes because of the movement of the tongue, lips, jaw and soft palate. However, there needs to be space inside the mouth to create an appropriate amount of oral resonance.

Allow your lower jaw to drop at its most natural point and use a mirror to look through to the back of the mouth. If you breathe through your nose and out through your mouth with your mouth still open, then you will see the action of the soft palate.

(c) **The nose (nasal resonator)**. There are two types of nasal resonance:

- when the vibrating column of air passes directly through the open soft palate to the nasal cavity: in English, this only happens on three sounds – 'm', 'n' and 'ng'.

- when the vibrating column of air does not pass directly into the nasal cavity, but instead pitches on to the hard palate just behind the upper teeth, the sound vibrations are carried through the bones of the hard palate to the nasal cavities. This type of nasal resonance can be heard in vowel sounds.

To produce the first type of nasal resonance, the soft palate must be in good working order; to produce the second type, there must be forward resonance (i.e. the breath force must be strong enough to bounce the sound off the hard palate).

If the speaker has a cold and the nasal cavities are blocked, there will not be any nasal resonance. If the soft palate does not close properly, too much nasal resonance will leak into the sound.

try this

Say 'mum', 'nose' and 'sing'. Repeat the words but this time while holding your nose. You should hear 'bub', 'dose' and 'sig' because there is no nasal resonance.

(d) **Balancing resonance**. Good resonance depends upon achieving a balance of vibration from the pharynx, mouth and nose. The quality of the sound will be affected if there is too much resonance from just one of the resonators.

When you practise your exercises, make sure that your spine is lengthened, your shoulders, neck and jaw are free from tension, and there is space inside your mouth and an adequate breath force to bring the sound forward. It is important that you try not to think about all of this when you are speaking or performing. You must practise your exercises so that it comes to you naturally.

The quality of sound will also be affected if the resonators are unhealthy (e.g. if you have a cold or sore throat). Unfortunately, there is little you can do to counteract the effects of illness on the quality of the sound.

Figure 3: The nose, mouth and pharynx

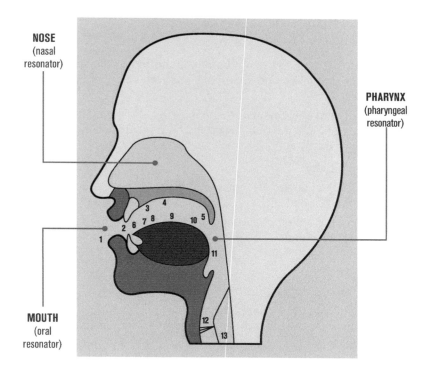

NOSE
(nasal
resonator)

PHARYNX
(pharyngeal
resonator)

MOUTH
(oral
resonator)

1 Lips   2 Teeth   3 Alveolar ridge   4 Hard palate   5 Soft palate
6 Tip of the tongue   7 Blade of the tongue   8 Front of the tongue
9 Centre of the tongue   10 Back of the tongue   11 Root of the tongue
12 Vocal cords or folds   13 Food passage

(e) **Head and chest resonance.** You may also feel vibrations from higher notes in your head and vibrations from lower notes in your chest when you speak; these are sometimes called 'head resonance' and 'chest resonance'. However, the head and chest are not official resonators because the vibrations come from sound waves produced by pharyngeal, oral and nasal resonance. For this reason, head and chest resonance are sometimes referred to as *secondary resonance*.

Basic speech production: Projection

Projection involves:

(a) **Audibility**

- Strong, secure breath (breath supported by the abdominal, diaphragmatic and intercostal muscles and released freely and easily)

- Forward placement of resonance (air and sound brought forward in the mouth, using the hard palate as a sounding board)

(b) **Intelligibility**

- Clarity of speech (tongue and lip muscularity; precise articulation)

- Appropriate emphasis and modulation (varying use of stress, volume, pace, pitch, inflection, tone colour and pausing, according to the thought and emotion being expressed)

(c) **Mental projection**

- Engaging the audience by commanding their attention, which ensures that the emotion of the words is conveyed clearly

Basic speech production: Articulation

A good speaker is a clear speaker. Take care not to run words into one another and make sure that you do not swallow word endings by speaking too quickly. Instead, the speaker should ensure that words and word endings are given the full weight of sound they deserve. Good diction means clear speech.

Articulation is the formation of clear and distinct sounds in speech.

Sound is turned into speech by the use of the organs of articulation. These are the tongue, the teeth, the teeth ridge, the lips and the hard and soft palates. A vowel sound is an unobstructed sound formed by the changing shape of the mouth. A consonant sound is an obstructed sound formed by two or more of the organs of articulation coming into contact with each other. Examples of this are the consonants 'b' and 'p', when the lips come into contact with each other, or 'f' and 'v', when the teeth touch the bottom lip.

Performance

Writing or reading a speech is different from performing a speech, as when performing you have to take into account that you will need to pause to take a breath. Understanding phrasing and pausing will help you understand when to take your breath and in turn will help with your performance.

Phrasing

Grammatically, a **phrase** is a group of two or more words within a sentence, that make sense. A phrase may not complete sense, on its own. For example:

The captain of the ship has gone on board.

Jack was found after a long search.

In speech, a **phrase** consists of a group of words linked together by sense. Phrases are sometimes called 'sense-groups'.

(a) **Sense-groups**. Each sense-group introduces a fresh idea. The sense-group may be one word or a number of words. To break a sense-group is to destroy the sense.

In *Death Rains* by Mary Ndlovu, we read:

Cool rain soaks down

Runs in streams,   [sense-group]

Awakening rivers.   [sense-group]

Laughter rings as

Children's play shapes

Dams and roads.   [sense-group]

(b) **Breath-groups**. Breath-groups and sense-groups frequently coincide, but this is not a rule. The breath-group represents the number of sense-groups that can easily be said in one breath. The ability to adjust breathing to meet the demands of the breath-group depends on an understanding of phrasing and breath control. Breath pauses may be longer than sense pauses and should occur where a longer pause is indicated by the text (often by punctuation, such as a comma or a full stop).

Notice how the breath-groups in *Death Rains* are slightly different from the sense-groups:

Cool rain soaks down

Runs in streams,

Awakening rivers.   [breath-group]

Laughter rings as

Children's play shapes

Dams and roads.   [breath-group]

(c) **Parenthesis**. Parenthesis occurs when a word, phrase or sentence is inserted, as an explanation, an afterthought or an aside into a passage which is grammatically complete without it. It is usually marked by brackets, dashes or commas. Parenthesis can be made clear in performance with a pause before and after the group of words, or with a change in pitch, pace or volume.

In *Through the Looking-Glass* by Lewis Carroll (1832–1898), there is a clear example of parenthesis – the phrase between the two commas:

"Some people," said Humpty Dumpty, looking away from her as usual, "have no more sense than a baby!"

Pausing

In speech, a **pause** is when sound stops. There are many different types of pause which help the speaker or reader to bring meaning and mood to life.

(a) **The sense pause**. The sense pause is used in connected speech to mark the sense by indicating the end or beginning of a sense-group. It is sometimes referred to as oral punctuation, but this can be misleading because it would seem to imply that it is used in the same places as written punctuation, which is not always the case.

(b) **The emphatic pause.** A pause for emphasis may be made before a word or phrase, after a word or phrase, or, for extra strong emphasis, both before and after a word or phrase. The word or phrase is, therefore, isolated and achieves prominence. Carefully timed, an emphatic pause will build suspense and climax. Holding an emphatic pause for too long will break the sense and alienate an audience.

Observe how effective an emphatic pause is when used before the final phrase of the extract from *Half Moon Investigations* by Eoin Colfer, when the speaker realises his mistake:

> *The window creaked open and a tremulous voice drifted down to me.*
>
> *"If you're looking for May Devereux, she lives next door."*
>
> *I was, of course, outside the wrong house.*

(c) **The emotional pause.** In an emotional pause the voice is suspended by the strong working of the emotions. It must be used with great subtlety or it will sound overdramatic and insincere.

In *Little Women* by Louisa May Alcott (1832–1888), there are several emotional pauses in the conversation between Jo and The Professor:

> *While Jo trudged beside him, feeling as if her place had always been there, and wondering how she ever could have chosen any other lot. Of course, she was the first to speak—intelligibly, I mean, for the emotional remarks which followed her impetuous "Oh, yes!" were not of a coherent or reportable character.*
>
> *"Friedrich, why didn't you..."*
>
> *"Ah, heaven, she gives me the name that no one speaks since Minna died!" cried the Professor, pausing in a puddle to regard her with grateful delight.*
>
> *"I always call you so to myself—I forgot, but I won't unless you like it."*

(d) **The rhythmical or metrical pause**. Rhythmical pauses are used at the ends of lines of verse and between stanzas to indicate the form and pattern of the verse. These pauses should be timed with the rhythm of the verse. A metrical pause is also used when a line of verse is shorter than the surrounding lines so that a pause is needed to balance the rhythm and timing.

Observe the rhythmical pauses in *Colonel Fazackerley* by Charles Causley (1917–2003):

> *Colonel Fazackerley Butterworth-Toast*
> [short pause]
>
> *Bought an old castle complete with a ghost,*
> [short pause]
>
> *But someone or other forgot to declare*
> [short pause]
>
> *To Colonel Fazack that the spectre was there.*
> [short pause]

(e) **The caesural pause**. A caesura is a slight pause which occurs mid-line in verse, usually indicated by a break in sense and sometimes indicated by a punctuation mark. This can be seen in *The Railway Children* by Seamus Heaney (1939–2013) in the middle of this stanza:

> *We were small and thought we knew nothing*
> *Worth knowing. We thought words travelled the wires*
> [caesural pause on full stop]
> *In the shiny pouches of raindrops,*

(f) **The suspensory pause**. A suspensory pause is indicated by no punctuation at the end of a line of verse, also known as an enjambed line. When it occurs in verse, the speaker needs to preserve the meaning without losing the rhythm or form of the verse. The last word of the first line is suspended by pitch and length; in other words, a pause on the word itself. Therefore, the speaker must continue on to the next line without a breath pause.

In the poem *Flight* by Joan Lees, several lines are enjambed and thus include a suspensory pause, as on the word 'splinters':

Circle the lake, sun splinters

on wooded shoreline and mountains.

Line structures in verse which affect pausing

(a) **End-stopping**. In an end-stopped line, the sense and rhythm fall silent, or pause, at the end of the line. This is often indicated by a punctuation mark.

(b) **Enjambment**. In an enjambed line, the sense of a line of verse continues on to the next line (the opposite of end-stopping).

 Select some poems/books/plays and find different examples of these definitions within the text.

Shakespeare

William Shakespeare was an English playwright, poet and actor; his work is still read, performed, studied and enjoyed by many people throughout the world today.

As we have used examples of Shakespeare's work throughout this publication to explain the structure and meaning of language, in this chapter we will briefly explore Shakespeare's style of writing and use of language. We will also look closely at a Shakespearean sonnet. For those who wish to read more about Shakespeare and his work, there are abundance of resources to choose from.

Shakespeare's style of writing

William Shakespeare wrote at a time when theatre in England was in its infancy but writing was established. His writing may have been influenced by the work of those who preceded him and by the customs of the time. For example, he may have read the early English sonnets of Henry Howard Earl and Thomas Wyatt; studied Latin; been familiar with Ancient Greek myths and been aware of the Ancient Greek rhythms.

When Shakespeare arrived in London, Christopher Marlowe (1564–1593) was a predominant playwright of the time. His plays, such as *The Tragical History of the Life and Death of Dr. Faustus* and *The Famous Tragedy of the Rich Jew of Malta,* used strong iambic pentameters in pairs of rhyming lines (couplets). This may have influenced Shakespeare, who also used iambic pentameter in his sonnets and plays.

We have already looked at rhythm in the chapter *Themes*, so
will not explore this again. We can see the use of iambic rhythm
in Shakespeare's work; for example, in *Macbeth* Act 2 Scene 2
when Macbeth says:

  o   –   o   –   o –   o   – o   –

But where   fore could not I pronounce   'Amen'?

(° represents a light stress and ‾ a heavy stress.)

Iambic pentameter is an especially good choice for a play
because we naturally speak in this rhythm. For example:

  o –   o   –   o   –   o – o   –

I'm go   ing to   the shop   to get   some bread.

(° represents a light stress and ‾ a heavy stress.)

  o   –   o   –   o   –   o   –   o –

That sun   shine is   so wel   come af   ter rain.

(° represents a light stress and ‾ a heavy stress.)

Shakespeare was able to develop the rhythm found in Marlowe's
work, possibly, as over time he found his own style. For example,
in early plays like *King Henry VI*, the iambic rhythm was fairly rigid
with quite a lot of rhyme, and lines were frequently end-stopped
by punctuation. By the time Shakespeare wrote *A Midsummer
Night's Dream*, the sense is flowing through to the next line
without a pause. An example of this is seen in Act 1 Scene 1
when Helena says:

I will go tell him of fair Hermia's flight:
Then to the wood will he, tomorrow night,
Pursue her; and for this intelligence
If I have thanks, it is a dear expense.

You will notice that the rhyming couplets are still evident, but a hierarchy of characters exist in this play. The characters, Titania, Oberon and Duke Theseus speak blank verse (iambic pentameter without rhyme); the four lovers speak mainly rhyming couplets; and the mechanicals (working class and comedic characters) speak mostly prose. This formula appears in many other plays and when Shakespeare varies this, there is always a reason. In this play, he even varies the iambic metre: Oberon and Puck both speak in trochaic tetrameter at times, as in the epilogue at the end of Act 5 Scene 1, when Puck says:

$$- \quad \circ \quad - \quad \circ \qquad - \quad \circ \quad - \qquad \circ$$

If we shadows   have off   en   ded,

(° represents a light stress and ‾ a heavy stress.)

$$- \quad \circ \quad - \quad \circ \qquad - \quad \circ \quad - \quad \circ$$

Think but this, and   all is mended.

(° represents a light stress and ‾ a heavy stress.)

The trochaic metre is the exact opposite of an iambic metre, with the stressed beat beginning at each foot.

These changes are very important for an actor to note, as it will assist them when performing one of Shakespeare's plays.

Here is a small selection of some other interesting variations found in Shakespeare's plays (an extensive selection is outside the scope of this book):

The Merchant of Venice

Shylock speaks prose when plotting against his Christian foes, but he speaks verse elsewhere.

Portia speaks verse except in some chatty, light-hearted scenes with her waiting gentlewoman Nerissa, where the words are not considered sufficiently important to merit verse.

Twelfth Night

In Act 1 Scene 5 the text changes midway from prose to verse. The move from prose into verse is first made by Viola when she praises Olivia's beauty, then gradually Olivia joins her in this transition. Olivia continues to speak in released blank verse, having fallen in love. Also within the play, love is presented through couples by the use of iambic pentameter.

Romeo and Juliet

The nurse alternates between using verse and prose according to her mood and the flippancy or seriousness of the topic.

King Lear

The fool speaks verse. All clowns and jesters in other plays speak prose. Shakespeare is making the point that this fool is a wise man who supports King Lear in his time of trial.

Othello

Iago speaks with Roderigo and Cassio in prose. We see him as an honest, direct soldier speaking to his colleagues, but in soliloquy his evil plans are delivered in blank verse. Here, the use of verse marks its importance to the plot.

Shakespeare's later tragedies and his final plays show the greatest variation in iambic verse. This development in the use of language marks Shakespeare out from his contemporaries.

In addition to his style of writing, Shakespeare used approximately 20,000 different words in his plays – a huge number at that time. He also introduced over 2,000 words that had never been seen in print before, such as: critical, extract, horrid, vast, excellent, barefaced, lonely, leapfrog and zany; and some of the most famous sayings in the English language originated in a Shakespearean play:

- All of a sudden – *The Taming of the Shrew*
- As luck would have it – *The Merry Wives of Windsor*
- At one fell swoop – *Macbeth*
- Fair play – *The Tempest*
- Good riddance – *Troilus and Cressida*
- Love is blind – *The Two Gentlemen of Verona, King Henry V* and *The Merchant of Venice*
- Wild goose chase – *Romeo and Juliet*.

Shakespeare's use of language

When examining Shakespeare's use of language it is important to remember that Shakespeare wrote his plays for the general public and not an academic audience. The audiences in public theatres, such as The Globe, were larger than those that are accommodated in today's theatres. Performances were not enhanced by lighting, design or scenery. Because of this we can infer that the people who attended performances did so for the content of the plays. The language of Shakespeare is designed to appeal to spectators in a theatre where the audience did not go to 'see' a play but to 'hear' one.

As Shakespeare's language is central to his plays, being aware of the kind of language his characters use can assist you with bringing a character to life. Shakespeare's language holds clues to the emotions the characters are feeling and can help you to make choices about how to proceed with your performance. By recognising the wordplay for what it is, a performer can make Shakespeare's words their own.

While exploring the language used by Shakespeare, we will look at wordplay, including some of the linguistic devices that are at the heart of Shakespeare's plays. Shakespeare uses linguistic devices, such as simile, metaphor, assonance, alliteration and imagery. We have already looked at rhythm, metre and controlling the flow of language in the chapter *Themes*, so we will not explore this again.

One of Shakespeare's earlier plays, *Romeo and Juliet*, shows some of the linguistic devices that Shakespeare used. Linguistic devices (figures of speech) are explained in the chapter *Figures of speech*.

Act 1 Scene 5 shows good use of **simile** and **metaphor**. In this scene, when Romeo sees Juliet for the first time at Capulet's ball, he admires her from a distance and says:

O, she doth teach the torches to burn bright.

It seems she hangs upon the cheek of night

As a rich jewel in an Ethiop's ear –

This simile compares Juliet to a valuable jewel shining against dark skin. Further on in the play, in Act 2 Scene 2, Romeo recklessly climbs over the wall into Capulet's orchard. As Juliet comes out onto her balcony, at first sight of her, he exclaims:

> *But soft, what light through yonder window breaks?*
> *It is the east and Juliet is the sun!*

This is a powerful metaphor, as the sun is the source of life, allowing the earth and all its inhabitants to survive. In the height of his rapture, this use of language tells us how passionately Romeo now loves Juliet. In the next line, Romeo introduces the 'envious moon' and so in two lines we have metaphor, **antithesis** and **personification** – as the moon cannot feel envy:

> *Arise fair sun and kill the envious moon*

Another famous example of Shakespeare's use of antithesis is in *King Richard III*; the opening lines of the play spoken by King Richard are:

> *Now is the winter of our discontent*
> *Made glorious summer by this sun of York,*

In *Romeo and Juliet*, Romeo enjoys exuberant use of wordplay and Juliet is his match. In Act 3 Scene 2, when Juliet learns that Romeo, now her husband, has killed her cousin, the violent Tybalt, in a duel, she uses **oxymoron** to describe her feelings. Juliet calls her new husband:

> *Beautiful tyrant, fiend angelical,*
> *Dove-feather'd raven, wolvish-ravining lamb!*

At the height of her grief and anger, Juliet uses complex, ornate imagery to express herself.

Shakespeare also uses **imagery** in his plays; for example, in *Othello*, Act 3 Scene 3, we see use of imagery when Iago describes jealousy:

> *It is the green-eyed monster, which doth mock*
> *The meat it feeds on.*

Other linguistic devices used by Shakespeare to emphasise his character's emotions are **alliteration**, **assonance** and **onomatopoeia**. Alliteration can be seen in *A Midsummer Night's Dream*, Act 2 Scene 1 when Titania says:

> *When we have laugh'd to see the sails conceive*
> *And grow big-bellied with the wanton wind;*

Assonance is particularly noticeable when the lines are spoken aloud; for example, in *Twelfth Night*, Act 1 Scene 5, Viola says:

> *Lady, you are the cruell'st she alive*
> *If you will lead these graces to the grave*
> *And leave the world no copy.*

Note that these lines also include the use of alliteration on the 'l' sounds, as well as further use of assonance in the words 'she', 'lead' and 'leave'.

Many examples of onomatopoeia can be found in Shakespeare's plays. For example, in *King Lear*, Act 3 Scene 2 we see King Lear addressing the storm:

> *Blow winds and crack your cheeks!*

King Lear articulates his own sense of disintegration by imitating the sound of the real storm using onomatopoeia. His words show violent sounds of distress, creating an impression of the interior confusion in his mind. As he continues to speak he encourages the actual storm to become ever more catastrophic and destructive:

> *You cataracts and hurricanoes, spout*
> *Till you have drenched our steeples, drowned the cocks!*
> *You sulphurous and thought-executing fires,*
> *Vaunt-couriers of oak-cleaving thunderbolts,*
> *Singe my white head! And thou, all-shaking thunder,*
> *Strike flat the thick rotundity o' the world,*
> *Crack nature's moulds, all germens spill at once*
> *That make ingrateful man!*

Another example of the effective use of language by Shakespeare can be seen when characters react to personal disaster. Within Shakespeare's plays, rather than bursting into tears, screaming or breaking down in speechless agony, Shakespeare's characters react to personal disaster by using speech to express their deepest feelings. Shakespeare's words should be spoken as they have been written. Form and structure should not to be broken by sobbing or long pauses and, above all, the words must be heard.

In Act 5 Scene 5 of *Macbeth*, Macbeth learns of the death of his wife. He greets the news without much surprise or any sense of personal sorrow. Instead, he speaks twelve lines of blank verse packed with figures of speech. Repetition, assonance, alliteration, extended use of metaphor and personification crowd in upon one another:

> *She should have died hereafter:*
> *There would have been a time for such a word. –*
> *To-morrow, and to-morrow, and to-morrow,*
> *Creeps in this petty pace from day to day,*
> *To the last syllable of recorded time;*
> *And all our yesterdays have lighted fools*
> *The way to dusty death. Out, out, brief candle!*
> *Life's but a walking shadow; a poor player,*
> *That struts and frets his hour upon the stage,*
> *And then is heard no more: it is a tale*
> *Told by an idiot, full of sound and fury,*
> *Signifying nothing.*

This famous speech makes a powerful point. The human reaction that we might expect from Macbeth at the news of his wife's death has been replaced by a weary cynicism, and such feelings that are now available to him are ones of a very particular despair. Life itself is absurd:

> *it is a tale*
> *Told by an idiot, full of sound and fury,*

There is no hope of any relief for him. His despair is absolute and the language tells us so.

Shakespeare's use of language can be seen when he moves from prose to verse and vice versa. This is a rhythmic change that should be noted by the performer. As we have seen earlier, when we first meet Countess Olivia in *Twelfth Night*, she speaks in prose, but as she falls in love with Cesario (Viola), her emotions lead her to make the transition into blank verse, and she remains speaking in this style for almost all of the remainder of the play.

We must, however, be careful not to generalise about the use of prose against the use of verse. In *As You Like It*, Phoebe is a shepherdess and expresses herself throughout the play in blank verse, whereas Audrey, another country girl, speaks only in prose. We should not assume that the working class and the comedic characters always speak in prose. Keeping an open mind and studying what is actually on the page will be the most helpful approach.

When studying and performing Shakespeare's plays understanding his language is crucial to understanding his characters. With his use of language, Shakespeare has already done much of the work for you.

The Shakespearean sonnet

We have already looked at the Shakespearean sonnet in our chapter *Figures of speech*, but we will explore the topic again in a little more depth.

Historical background

The roots of the English sonnet can be traced back to two young courtiers – Sir Thomas Wyatt and Henry Howard – at the court of Henry VIII – Sir Thomas Wyatt and Henry Howard (see chapter *Themes*). These two courtiers introduced into the English court the styles and metrical rhythm of Italian humanist poets. In doing so, they laid the foundations from which English poetry, and specifically the sonnet, could flourish.

As a sonneteer, Wyatt focused his poetry on the themes of courtly love and ill-treatment at the hands of his lovers – this set the tone for the subject matter of the English sonnet, including those of Shakespeare. Howard's use of the rhyming scheme – abab cdcd efef gg – was later taken up by Shakespeare in his work. In this rhyming scheme, we recognise three quatrains and a rhyming couplet.

Themes of Shakespeare's sonnets

The main theme running through Shakespeare's sonnets is that of love in various forms, from enchantment to disenchantment. A careful reading of Shakespeare's sonnets reveals three underlying themes. These themes are:

- <u>Time</u>: the brevity of life's span
- <u>Beauty</u>: both physical beauty and the process of ageing
- <u>Desire</u>: the desire for a loved one.

Shakespeare's sonnets formed an opus of 154. To understand the sonnet form we will look at one of Shakespeare's sonnets – *Sonnet 75*.

If we divide Shakespeare's sonnets into three basic groups, *Sonnet 75* falls within those addressed to a young man, which form sequence 1–126. The sonnets in sequence 127–152 look at the 'dark lady' and the opus ends with two sonnets devoted to the love god Cupid.

Sonnet 75

First quatrain			
So are you to my thoughts as food to life,	a	(line 1)
Or as sweet seasoned showers to the ground;	b	(line 2)
And for the peace of you I hold such strife	a	(line 3)
As 'twixt a miser and his wealth is found:	b	(line 4)

Second quatrain			
Now proud as an enjoyer, and anon	c	(line 5)
Doubting the filching age will steal his treasure;	d	(line 6)
Now counting best to be with you alone,	c	(line 7)
Then bettered that the world may see my pleasure;	d	(line 8)

Third quatrain			
Sometime all full with feasting on your sight,	e	(line 9)
And by and by clean starved for a look,	f	(line 10)
Possessing or pursuing no delight	e	(line 11)
Save what is had, or must from you be took.	f	(line 12)

Rhyming couplet			
Thus do I pine and surfeit day by day,	g	(line 13)
Or gluttoning on all, or all away.	g	(line 14)

The sonnet consists of three quatrains: the first quatrain sets up the situation in the poet's mind; the second develops it; and the third (from line nine) opens with what is called 'a turn' in a sonnet. This is sometimes shown by the introduction of 'but'; this is when the poet offers a change of mind or argument. In this sonnet, the turn occurs in line nine, but this can happen on a different line.

The sonnet ends with a rhyming couplet, which adds an antithetical farce to the evaluation of the poet's emotions that it encapsulates.

Within this sonnet, at first it appears that the young man will be stolen from the sonneteer simply for a sexual relationship – the object of 'love' will be 'filched' by another – but as the sonnet continues we discover that this is not the case.

Within the sonnet we see the use of antithesis (see lines three and eleven) and metaphor mentions five of the deadly sins: avarice, gluttony, pride, lust and envy.

Preparing to speak a sonnet

When preparing to recite the sonnet, you should first seek to discover what emotional tone can be found – in *Sonnet 75* on careful reading joy, pain, frustration, confusion and denial can all be discovered.

Recognise that Shakespeare has carefully chosen the words and images of the sonnet form, as he only has fourteen lines to show his reflective emotions (and purpose) to the listener. When reading the sonnet, you must follow the thoughts of the poet, as the structure suggests. The sonnet form is an evocation of at least four thought patterns, not just one.

As part of your preparation, and so that you obtain a feel for the sonnet, each sonnet should be scanned before reading it. When reading the sonnet:

- note how the iambic rhythm predominates and where the irregularities in this rhythmical structure fall
- ask why Shakespeare introduces a strong spondee (a metrical foot consisting of two long syllables) that changes the metrical pattern
- look for the internal rhymes in the sonnet; is there repetition, alliteration, assonance?

When speaking the sonnet, it should not be 'belted out' in a thoughtless manner and you must be sensitive to motive and tone. Only when you identify with the mind of the poet can you find his 'voice' and replicate the emotional tones that are inherent in the phrase patterns.

The Elizabethan Theatre

When reading Shakespeare's plays, it's worth considering the theatres that these plays would have been performed in, as this is a consideration that Shakespeare may have taken in to account when writing his plays.

Theatre design in Shakespeare's day conformed to three broad types: inn yards, open-air amphitheatres and hall theatres. We will look at each type of theatre in turn.

The inn yards

The inn yards was the name given to private inns where plays were performed. Plays could either be performed inside the inn or in the yard.

The audience capacity for these plays was small, with no more than 500 spectators.

The players usually rented the space from the inn's landlord and income from performances was typically made by asking the spectators for a monetary contribution.

Examples of inn yard theatres included The Bull Inn, The White Hart and The Bell.

In 1595, a ban on performances in city inns paved the way for amphitheatres and hall theatres.

The open-air amphitheatre

The Globe is the most famous example of an open-air amphitheatre. It was built in the common design of the time – a circular, timber-built structure, which was open to the skies, with three tiers of seating within and a thatched roof above. There were doorways to both the left and right side of the stage, through which actors could make their entrances and exists. The modern reconstruction on the South Bank of the River Thames reflects this.

Spectators paid a penny to stand and watch the play from the pit (the central space within the theatre). There were also seats for spectators at the side of the stage, which cost sixpence.

The audience capacity of a theatre such as The Globe would have been around 3,000, roughly double the capacity of the modern reconstruction.

The early amphitheatre playhouses included The Red Lion and James Burbage's The Theatre.

The hall theatres

Hall theatres were also known as private playhouses and came into use about ten years after the first public amphitheatre playhouses. They were adapted from existing buildings and differed in three key respects:

- The cost of admission was greater; the minimum price paid was sixpence. This effectively priced the poorest spectators out and gained hall theatres a reputation as an upmarket alternative to public amphitheatre playhouses.

- They were indoor spaces without standing room. The pit area was filled with benched seating and flanked by galleries of seats on different levels. Hence, while the number of spectators was reduced, the higher admission cost compensated for this. Blackfriars was the most famous hall theatre.

- The cheapest seats in hall theatres were furthest from the stage and the most expensive seats were near to or on the stage. This feature of the hall theatres is one that endures today in modern performance venues.

One hall theatre, the Blackfriars Theatre, was purchased by James Burbage in 1596. However, he was barred from playing there when wealthy residents of the district complained about potential noise and traffic congestion. In 1599 Burbage's sons, Richard and Cuthbert, dismantled the theatre and rebuilt it on Bankside, as The Globe. They funded the project by offering shares in the building to five leading players of the time, and Shakespeare was one of these players. Arguably, Shakespeare wrote his greatest plays from 1599 onwards; perhaps because he had a real stake in the success of his company. It is possible that without this case of 'nimbyism' in 1596, theatrical history would have been very different.

Shakespeare's company acquired use of the Blackfriars Theatre in 1609 and performed there in the winter months. They performed at The Globe in the summer months.

Other hall theatres include The Cockpit and Salisbury Court.

Performance considerations

Performance considerations that prevailed in Shakespeare's day were different from those we see today. For instance, women were not permitted to perform on stage, and so female characters would have been acted by boys whose voices had not yet broken.

Understanding the practical approach that Shakespeare's actors would have adopted in performance is an inexact science, but contemporary sources allow us to reconstruct some of the considerations faced by performers in a playhouse. By studying these considerations, as well as by looking at some internal evidence within Shakespeare's own plays, we can make some tentative, but reasonably informed, guesses as to how these considerations could have affected the players' approach to their roles.

One performance consideration for actors of the time is the conduct of the audience. It is assumed that in Elizabethan (and Jacobean) theatres, the audiences would have been vocal in their appreciation and disapproval of the performance, and frequent contemporary references to 'mewing' and hissing attests to this fact. There is perhaps a hint of the challenges that players could expect to face from a hostile crowd in the Prologue of *King Henry V* when the chorus concludes their opening speech with a plea to the audience:

> *Gently to hear, kindly to judge our play.*

Another consideration for those on stage would have been the constant churn in the crowd caused by the need to exit and re-enter the theatre in the event of needing the toilet. Due to this an impression of the theatre forms as one with a lively, bustling, possibly raucous atmosphere.

Performers would also have had to contend with both background noise from the audience and the acoustics of the theatre itself. In particular, the yard and amphitheatre playhouses were open to the skies and would have demanded considerable vocal power from the actors, who would need to retain spectators' attention. For the same reasons, the actors would probably have adopted an interactive style with the audience. One can infer from Shakespeare's plays that a lot of indicative physical gesturing would have been employed to engage the audience. For example, the Prologue in *King Henry V* mentions:

> *The flat unraised spirits that hath dared*
> *On this unworthy scaffold to bring forth*
> *So great an object. Can this cockpit hold*
> *The vasty fields of France?*

From Shakespeare's plays we can also infer that these gestures were sometimes overdone; for example, in *Hamlet*, Act 3 Scene 2, Hamlet advises a group of visiting players:

> *Nor do not saw the air too much with your hand, thus, but use all gently;*

The same speech by Hamlet goes on to suggest that vocal delivery could become overwrought:

O, it offends me to the soul to hear a robustious periwig-pated fellow tear a passion to tatters, to very rags, to split the ears of the groundlings, who for the most part are capable of nothing but inexplicable dumb-shows and noise.

It is also assumed that ad-libbing was employed by actors of the time, especially comic actors, and this is hinted at in *Hamlet,* Act 3 Scene 2, when Hamlet urges the players:

And let those that play your clowns speak no more than is set down for them

Some scholars speculate that the plays would have been performed at a fairly fast-paced rate since numerous sources suggest that performances did not exceed two hours in duration; for example, the Prologue to *Romeo and Juliet* mentions the:

Two hours' traffic of our stage

Also bear in mind that during the winter months daylight would have been spent by approximately four o'clock, so this imperative and the length of many plays would have allowed little time for the luxury of dramatic pause.

A further consideration for Shakespearean actors would have been the number of plays they performed each month, which could have been as many as fifteen.

Consider, in addition, the facts that many plays featured elaborate swordplay in both duel and group combats and that many plays concluded with a lively jig by the cast, and you can begin to appreciate the wide range of mental, vocal and physical skills required of Shakespeare's players and those of other companies.

Acknowledgements

All references to acts, scenes, lines and dates of Shakespearean plays are as set out in: Proudfoot, R., Thompson, A. and Kastan D. S. (ed.) (2015) *Shakespeare Complete Works*, Revised Edition, India: The Arden Shakespeare, an imprint of Bloomsbury Publishing PLC.